DAILY SIPS:

Dreams Fulfilled Purposely

Vol. 1

Angela Davie

authorHOUSE®

AuthorHouse™
1663 Liberty Drive
Bloomington, IN 47403
www.authorhouse.com
Phone: 1-800-839-8640

Published by AuthorHouse 05/27/2014

ISBN: 978-1-4969-1550-4 (sc)
ISBN: 978-1-4969-1549-8 (e)

CONTENTS

ACKNOWLEDGMENTS

I would like to thank my Father, God and Savior Jesus Christ for loving me as I am.

I know that I am a continual work in process, as I am and have been kept to seize my ordained purpose.

To all those who assisted me with Spoken Word Nights, Lajuane, Deaconess Ava, Deaconess Lisa, Charday, Minister Sherry, my sister Lena. To Pastor Everrit, and Pastor Sann Whiteside as they allowed me to use Higher Praise Covenant Church, while also inspiring me to fulfill my purpose in the writing of this book. To Reggie, I appreciate all of your support, through the process of Spoken Word.

To Ms Carol thanks for seeding a writing journal into my life.

To my father Nehemiah thanks for helping me as I regained my ground

To my daughter Ashley you are my greatest accomplishment!

To William my significant other, you are a great distinguished man of Honor! Thanks for all your encouragement, through the beginning and the completion of this book.

To Pastor Jeff my Best Friend who was and is Always there for me, I am so thankful for you.

To Tiff thanks for your humor that warms my soul

To my sister Vanessa, and brother Bobby, and sister Pam, I love you guys

To Roselyn, thanks for giving me my first professional speaking engagement at the "Grand Affair"

To Liqua, you are the best God given daughter ever

To the McDonald's Crew, thanks for being like fathers toward me

To my work posse, I treasure you all it's a privilege to work with all of you.

To all those who are attached to me, Grandma Mary, Grandma Parks Aunties, Uncles, cousins, nephews, nieces, God children, friends, etc, I love you all!

Also, last but not least to my all my deceased loved ones, all of you are forever in my heart. Grandma and Mom thanks for being all that you were.

DEDICATION

This book is dedicated to all the dreamers, who are in pursuit of their purpose. Ascend to your rightful place in life, as you believe you were Destined to Achieve your Purposeful Dreams!

INTRODUCTION

"Daily Sips Volume One, Dreams Fulfilled Purposely is a motivational, inspiring composite, poetic book that will project people to seek their specific purpose in life. As, passionate inner dreams indicate their starting route. Purpose begets purpose, become a witness, so that others can believe to become!"

Angela Davie

A DREAM IS........

A dream is an escape from the ordinary to the extraordinary

A dream is an oasis, while one endures pit stops

A dream is an illumination that defies the greatest obstacles

A dream is like a magnet, as it beckons one to charge

A dream is likened to a resuscitator, as it breathes vitality
into a weary soul

A dream is an opportunity to experience a remarkable life

A DREAM'S COURSE

The steps to any dream are likened to mountain cliffs

It is easy to dream big

However, it is much harder to endure a dream's ruggedness

As, a dream is embarked doubt and fear diminish gradually

The course of any dream lifts limitations, as it permits the soul to emerge

Dreams groom the world, as those who once beheld them gain their occupancy

A dream's course chisels mundane lives into beautiful masterpieces

Follow your dream's course!

WHAT IS LIFE WITHOUT DREAMS?

Life without dreams is meaningless and void

Life without dreams is pointless and aimless

Life without dreams is reckless and regretful

Life with a dream turns the fearful into the fearless

Life with a dream brings a beam of hope to the most hopeless situations

Life with a dream transforms the unimaginable to a definite reality

Live your dreams to life!

THE TRUTH OF A DREAM

The truth of a dream lies in the corridors of one's soul

The truth of a dream reveals direction, as it dispels twisted paths

The truth of a dream will broaden eyes to believe

Accept your truthful dream, as you aspire to its destined height!

PURPOSELY BEAUTIFUL

The beauty of purpose denotes freedom

The beauty of purpose restores joy to a downcast heart

The beauty of purpose ignites one's soul to claim its absolute purpose

The beauty of purpose exemplifies all who regard its splendor

The beauty of purpose recognized allows all to catch their dreams

NEVER LET IT BE EASY

It is so easy to give up, and call your dreams insane

It is so easy to give up, and cast unwarranted blame

It is so easy to give up, and say there is no use

It is so easy to give up, when there is a constant excuse

It is so easy to give up, when distractions come our way

It is so easy to give up, but remember dreams are fulfilled
by consciously living and doing each day

Do not let the ease of easy push your dreams away

BREATHE, FOR YOUR PURPOSE

When thoughts of discouragement intrude your heart and mind

Breathe, and listen for the truth

When it seems like your present position is your only destined height

Breathe, and listen for the truth

Opposition is the foe of all who are moving toward their purpose

BREATHE, as you believe continuously through disbelief; your thoughts will promote or tear down your dreams

THE WEIGHT OF THE WAIT

The wait and weight of a deferred dream can cripple one's spirit if allowed

The wait and weight of a dream will induce much anxiety at times

The weight of the wait, regarding your dream is purposed to build character and humility

Through the wait and weight of your dream exercise patience, as you continually remind yourself the weight will be worth your wait eventually

THE WEIGHT OF YOUR WAIT IS BRINGING ABOUT THE UNSEEN

KEEP YOUR DREAMS AWAKE!

The awakening of a dream within a soul, reestablishes the meaning for one to be planted in the world

Dreams focus us to live above the norm

Dreams bring out our creativity, as we indulge their existence into form

Dreams hold our imaginations captive in the present, as we work them into fruition

Dreams awaken the young, older, and those that are in between

Sleep no more, and become that which you have dreamed!

PUSH AHEAD

There is a future ahead, where your dream is awaiting your arrival

Push steadily toward it and lose not your attention

Time will bring many congratulations; you will do well

As, the feet of the wise are always in pursuit to excel

Stay committed to the passion of your dream that burns within

Allow thankfulness to continually overshadow your heart

As, you are expecting your purposeful-built end

Keep your head clear from discouragement, when it seems your dream cannot come true

Push ahead, and believe your dream is an actuality for you!

THE SPORTING OF LIFE

The long jump, began before one accelerated with speed

The winning touchdown was ran before one's cleats crossed
the end zone

The dunk of a lifetime, was slammed before a player
gripped the ball

The homerun of the inning, was swung before a batter ever
grabbed a bat

The tape at the finish line was broke, before a runner began
the race

The sporting of life also renders the same; we get what we
give, like athletes in their game

SEIZE YOUR DREAMS LIKE AN ATHLETE!

THE WISDOM OF A DREAMER

A day of a wise dreamer goes beyond wishing, as they do to achieve

A wise dreamer knows that wishful thoughts will not bring a dream to pass

Wise dreamers think, plan and seek their routes, as they perform confirming belief

Dreams are projected from the soul, as it seeks its earthly positioning

Be a wise dreamer, and put your thoughts to the test

Are you casually dreaming; or will your dreams manifest?

THE SPIRIT OF A CHAMPION

The Spirit of a Champion avails above obstacles seen and unseen

The Spirit of a Champion realizes that everyone will not understand their predestined route

The Spirit of a Champion never focuses on the hurdles of life

But, The Spirit of a Champion will roar in seemingly times of defeat

The Spirit of a Champion will not be broken; they always match what they meet

Thus, The Spirit of a Champion will never dismiss their innate dream

The Spirit of a Champion will follow its dream's obstacle course until the end!

Presently Now

It is very hard to stay focused in the present, as one is eager to reside in the brightness of their future

It is very hard to do what is needed in the now; however present preparation reaps future benefits

It is hard to appreciate the matters at hand, as one anticipates the pleasurable moments to come

But, commit to your present works, as they will be bridges to your future

WILL TO DO!

If you cannot love yourself with little, you will not be able to honor yourself with much

If you cannot accept where you are in life now, you will not be able to handle the waves of advancement

If you cannot applaud yourself in your present state, then you will never be able to truly celebrate yourself in your future

If you cannot you will not

WILL TO DO!

GOALS THAT ARE SEEN IN THE MIND

Goals that are seen in the mind, propel us to fly toward their existence

Goals that are seen in our mind, challenge us to override thoughts of mediocrity

Goals that are seen in the mind, penetrate space and time

Goals that are seen in the mind, embody the identity of one's soul, as they are drawn into realities

CAPTURE YOUR GOALS IN YOUR MIND!

THE HUNGER OF PURPOSE

If purpose is not engaged it will tug and harass the soul

The Hunger of Purpose cries, and screams demanding to be fed, likened to new born babies thrusting their voices out of hunger

The Hunger of Purpose will not be quieted

The Hunger of Purpose will stalk until death

Its sole desire is to persuade one to fulfill the entirety of their existence

The hunger of purpose is fed through people seizing their dreams, as they begin to embrace its URGING to become

This is the Purpose of the Hunger!

THE MIND OF YOUR WILL

The will of the mind for good, changes one way streets to highways of opportunities

The will of the mind for good, wields closed doors to swing open, while disengaging their hinges

The will of the mind for good, ensures dreams their clearance for flight

The will of the mind for good is likened to valuable resources that sustain us all

The will of the mind for good, destroys barriers that appear to obstruct destinies

Will Your Mind To Do!

THE PURSUIT OF DEFINED PURPOSE

Why should one strategize, mentally and physically to obtain the purpose of their soul?

Purpose produces a magnitude of energy, which constantly recharges the soul, as it steadily obtains maximization

Many have expended their time on foolish pursuits, instead of pursuing their defined purpose

Found purpose quenches the soul's innate desire to avail

If purpose is not found, there is an insatiable longing that looms until death

The pursuit of your defined purpose is crucial to your well-being!

THE REACH OF PURPOSE

Purpose is not reached by wishing that all your dreams will come true

Purpose is not reached by mimicking what others say or do

Purpose is not reached without thought of the mind and or action of the feet

Purpose is reached by those who declare, they are strong and not miserably weak

Purpose is reached as one accepts their wealthy inner core, as their heart, mind and soul Collaborate to Soar!

THE ROAD....

The road to your destiny was designed just for you

It may seem unbearable at times, as you continually meet its curves

But, do not stray from its winding or narrowness

Surely on its end there is the destination called Blessedness

EMBRACE YOUR ROAD!

THE SEASONS OF TIME

The future is a place that one should not rush to see

However, it must be taken very seriously, as it holds one's
spot where they were intended to be

Yet, the past, present and future all hold their respectable place;
in each we play our role, as the constant recipients of grace

The beauty of these three seasons will bring much revelation
to the soul

Treasure them entirely, as in each, wisdom will unfold

The present will lead you to your future, as the past is swept
away

**Remember, you cannot celebrate one season over the
other, because they all started, and will start as a day**

THE ABSENT PAST

My past seemed impossible to live through, but I knew my future was bright

My past was dark as night, but my future I knew was full of light

My past weighed me down

My future had me lifted up

My past tried to kill me, but my future kept calling my name

Live life present to future, and let the past sleep away

REGAINING GROUND

There are many dreams in the hearts of those, who were severely wounded in their youth

Broken, bent, and bruised within; they seek meaning for their significant worth

However, their pierced wings keep them from taking flight

Only divine purpose can mend the wings of the wounded, as it leads and guides healing wrongs into rights

Some wounded souls pursue vain ambition to seal their wings

But, the purpose within dreams is the only balm for the wings of the wounded; as they retrieve their wholeness in their esteemed being

Regain and Fly!

IF........

If I am, so shall I be

If I acknowledge, so then shall I see

If I realize, so then shall I accept

If I seek the truth in all situations, then shall I stand free!

IF.....

THE ACCEPTANCE OF YOU!

You are not below anyone, although others may look down on you

You are not less than anyone, although some may try to subtract your worth

You are not destined to fail, so stop rehearsing that line

You are a product of greatness, realize this and make the most of your time

You are capable to do whatever good that themes your soul

The Acceptance of You will always keep you whole!

THE ANSWERS THAT BE!

Where can one find their purpose?

In the voice of one's own soul

How can one know what their purpose is?

A person's purpose fits them exclusively, as they attend to its functioning

How can purpose be obtained?

It is grasped within, as one follows the design of their inner wiring

How can one know if they are aligned with their purpose?

Destined purpose quiets the spirit, while freeing the soul

As, it directs one toward their ultimate functioning

The answers that be are able to flow without any stagnation, as one interlocks with their purpose

THE DEBT OF PURPOSE

The debt to one's self is to become the purpose of one's own specific design

The debt of purpose, demands different obligations from each individual, which is contingent on their unique course

To pay off one's debt with surety, one must make payments of wisdom, dedication, truth, and love to themselves

The debt of purpose cannot be bankrupted, one must adhere to its set costs, or they will undergo a nagging pain due to nonperformance

No one can be forced to contribute to the fulfillment of their purpose

Hence, only fulfilled purpose will bring harmony to a chaotic soul

Make daily installments toward your **Debt of Purpose!**

THE DEPTH OF BECOMING

The depth of becoming, what one was designed to be stretches the soul to reach unreachable heights

It calls deeply, even if one has subconsciously given up their right to become

The depth of becoming draws the soul from its mediocre comfort zone

It leads the soul to its designated position, so that it may bloom

The depth of becoming is innate, as we all were constructed to shine

Thus, there should never be any competition of light against light

The depth of becoming is a soulful journey that anchors us in our divine purpose

Become all that is Deep within You!

THE GREAT IN YOU!

Greatness is in you, there is no need to pursue it

Greatness is not something that you need to achieve

Greatness is displayed, as you acknowledge your own
personal worth

Greatness is not something that we speak with

Greatness is something that we confirm

The Greatness in you, must be lived out to the max

The Greatness in You shall never be held back!

WHO AM I?

I am me, and I can only be me

Who am I?

I am someone that is worthy of respect and honor

Who am I?

I am someone that has a purpose that will be manifested in the earth

Who am I?

I am a competent individual that is grateful to be me

Who am I?

A Thriving Person, as I Seize All I was Intended to Be!

WHO SAID?

Who said you are not able to achieve the yearnings within your soul?

Who said you cannot accomplish the dreams that have engulfed your heart?

Who said that you are wasting your time pursuing what gives a spark to your life?

Permit no one to question your dreams!

WORTH....

The worth of people never goes down, as with stock though some would argue this case

The worth of people is never determined by where they work, live, and or spend their days

The true worth of people is configured within their own individual souls

Yet, only the wise realize this, as their lives they compose

The weight of your worth is not what you will ever do

The weight of your worth resides solely in You!

WHAT THE AVERAGE EYES CANNOT SEE

You are more than what the average eyes can see

You could function at a higher level, if you choose to believe

You have to consciously ENCOURAGE yourself to achieve great feats

While, you stand up deep down inside, as you never retreat

It is not the power of a man or woman that keeps them on their designated path

But, the acknowledgement of their inner worth, as they refuse to be defined by their past

Know your worth from the sight of your own soul, as you disregard what others deem

WALK!

If I walk alone, I can still make my way

If I walk alone, I still can seize each day

If I walk alone, I must never stay despaired

If I walk alone, I must embrace the essence of me

If I walk alone, I still can achieve

I will walk alone at times, yet I will continually believe

HOPE TO SEE!

See the present beauty of life, as it offers glimpses of hope

Hope sees beyond the condition of any matter

Hope sees when others disbelieve

Hope sees when the odds are against it

Hope sees through the darkest days

Always Hope to See!

THE HOPE OF HOPE

Hope revokes all residual stains, so the mind may thrive unhindered

Hope is the miracle of thought, as it transforms old thinking processes

Hope reveals lighted paths to future successes

Hope motivates one to ignore stigmas, as they rise above its ignorance

The question is never where one has been, but how far one is willing to believe they can ascend

HOPE SUSTAINS LIFE

OUR PILLAR HOPE

Hope is the foundation of strength, which supersedes the darkest day

Hope is the pillar which holds the weight of the world, so that one's spirit is not crushed

Hope is the shelter which encourages the soul to continually endure, as it is continuously exposed to the weathering of life

HOPE!

DOORS

A door will never open if another is not closed

Another door will not just open on its own, it is willed open by preparation

Open and closed doors come to those who are not idle in their heart or mind

Open and closed doors will get one intentionally to their respective place in due time

Closed doors should never be discouraging, as open doors should never be taken for granted

POSSIBLY!

The worst of a situation is possibly the best situation,
because it is there where maturation evolves

The best of times could possibly be the worst of times,
because complacency might sneak in

The light of day is more brilliant than a day of light,
because revelation pierced denials grips

The end of some thoughts awaken the soul to bloom, as
weights are exchanged for wings

The initial perception of a matter cannot guarantee an outcome

Many words will not bring something to pass

Yet, actions breed the fulfillment of words hastened

THE TICK OF TIME

We are all on the time clock of life, as we continue to live enduring each new day

So, we must seize the best of our worth by refusing all self-induced delays

The youth, middle aged and the young at heart all suffer the same

Facing the continuous race against time, as its hands constantly slip away

Past, Present and Future life is tick, tick, ticking away

Yet, time just measures our moments, as we all find our individual way

See your dreams as you become them!

WEALTHY MOMENTS

Moments are fleeting just ask the old

Moments are markers that the future will hold

Moments are seized, and appropriated by those who are bold

Moments are expenditures, as they are counted up as costs

People who misuse them will suffer great loss

Moments are sometimes never valued until their actually blown away, make sure you take advantage of them each and every day!

DAYS

Everyday will bring an opportunity to change your position in life

Do you desire to advance from your present position?

If so, realize that each new day if handled properly is a footprint toward your expanded life

The days will seem long, if you are not aligning yourself with your purpose

So, take each day responsibly celebrate your now, as you are preparing for your future

Keep your mind clear from complaints, as you seek positive ways

Know that your future is contained, upon how you are living out your pre-existing days

Do Your Days with Your Purpose in Mind!

THE DOING OF THE WISE

We all have to do time in life

The goal is making every moment productive

There are so many distractions that vie for our time

Hence, we must focus on the things that will elevate our being

Time is the subject of life, as we become wise students of its course

As, we respect it as precious by honoring its great worth

STEPS

The steps toward any dream are likened to mountain cliffs

It is easy to dream big

However, it is much harder to stay steadfast

The steps of a focused dream illuminate the soul of a pursuer, as it gives inspiration to live

So, keep stepping high, as you continue attending your dream

THE ENEMY IN YOU!

Always remember, you are your own worst enemy

No one has the ability to determine your destined height

You are your own worst enemy the main one that can thwart your future's plans

However, people will try to block you with the intention of ultimately stopping you

But, it all remains the same

You are and will be your own worst enemy; no one will ever have a greater claim!

THE WISDOM OF NEVER

Never measure yourself to another, because it is absolutely impossible to compare invaluable against invaluable

Never dismiss yourself, by falsely believing that another is better than you

Never desire to be in someone else's place, because you would not be able to handle what it takes to be them

Never allow anyone to stay in your life that discourages your person

Never become so engrossed with yourself, and forget perfection is an unobtainable feat

Never seek to force others to like or accept you, because you will always be pining for their approval

Never forget the Wisdom of Never

DO NOT ENTERTAIN JEALOUSY

Jealousy is never becoming, let it not adore your crown

If it is given a small space in your heart, it will attempt to bring you down

It tries to play us all against each other, by comparing our strengths and weaknesses

It highlights what others have, as well as what they are doing; it will diminish your position if you look through its eyes

Jealousy's goal is to magnify the lives of some, while misleading others into thinking that their lives are insignificant

If you believe jealousy's hype, it will leave you empty and bitter

Jealousy binds the mind from true sight, as it emphasizes lies

It turns people against people, as their own hearts they begin to despise

Jealousy unchecked deceives many lives!

GIVE THANKS

As you are swimming toward your dreams, give a breath of thanks

As you are swinging toward your dreams, give a wave of thanks

As you are walking toward your dream, give a stride of thanks

As you are leaping toward your dreams, give a jump of thanks

A thankful heart carries a dream!

CAN'T BE STOPPED

Are you aware that no one can stop your dreams, regardless of what they say or do?

So, think and focus keep your mind stayed on truths

Fight with wisdom toward those who do not believe

Yet, do not ever use fists or ill words; they could possibly kill your dreams

Beware, there are many dream killers roaming, severely damaged and bitter within

Seek not their friendship, because in their hearts you cannot win

They hate hope, as they are void of its believing power

Dream killers desire to steal the hope of others, as their goal is to devour

Guard your hope, as you allow them no access to mire your dreams

Your dreams are seeds that others will perch on one day

YOU CANNOT BE STOPPED!